Learn While You Scrub
Science in the Tub

James Lewis
Illustrated by Joe Greenwald

 Meadowbrook Press

Distributed by Simon & Schuster
New York

Library of Congress Cataloging-in-Publication Data

Lewis, James, 1943–
    Learn while you scrub: science in the tub.
    p.   cm.
    Summary: Illustrated instructions for a variety of simple
scientific experiments that can be done in the sink or bathtub.
        1. Science—Experiments—Juvenile literature.
[1. Science—Experiments. 2. Experiments.] I. Greenwald, Joe,
ill. II. Title.
Q164.L48   1989   507.8—dc20   89-33793
ISBN:0-88166-172-4

Editors: Katherine Stevenson and Lisa Oelfke
Production Editor: Sandy McCullough
Production Manager: Pam Scheunemann
Designer: Cathy Cullinane-Skraba
Illustrator: Joe Greenwald

S&S Ordering #: 0-671-68999-1

Published by Meadowbrook Press, 18318 Minnetonka Boulevard, Deephaven, MN 55391.

BOOK TRADE DISTRIBUTION by Simon & Schuster, a division of
Simon and Schuster, Inc., 1230 Avenue of the Americas, New
York, NY 10020.

89 90 91 92 5 4 3 2 1

Printed in the United States of America.

To my wife, Nancy,
and my two children,
Tiffany and Jared.

Contents

Preface vi

Acknowledgments vii

Making Bathtime Safe viii

A Note to Parents ix

List of Materials x

Basic Activities 1

    The Unsinkables 2

    Shipshape! 4

    Building a Raft 6

    Measuring Up 8

    Let's Swing 10

    The Sprinkler 12

    Pump It Up 14

    The Magic Straw 16

    The Lidless Bottle 18

    Upside-Down Magic 20

    Dry-Paper Mystery 22

    Push and Pull 24

    Stick with Me! 26

    How Strong Is Water? 28

    Magic Comb 30

    Disappearing Act 32

    Hang It Up 34

    Was I That Dirty? 36

    Mystery Ice 38

Advanced Activities **41**

What's Inside? 42

Weigh It 44

On the Level..46

All Stopped Up 48

Waterwheel Power...50

Soap-Powered Boat 52

The Riverboat 54

Two-Straw Magic 56

Blow It Up...58

Just Drifting Along...60

They're Only Bubbles 62

Deep-Sea Diver 64

The Big Squeeze..66

A Little Hole 68

Stop the Leak 70

Catching Bubbles 72

Bubble Chains..74

Siphon Secrets 76

Up the Wall...78

Cloth Siphon 80

String Me Along 82

Look Again 84

Preface

Bathtime can be a wonderful time for young children, a time for play, fun, and relaxation. It can be special for parents, too, providing a chance to talk and share with their children at the end of the day. Many parents value the special nature of bathtime and try to enrich it with colorful toys, bubble baths, and washable dolls.

This book is dedicated to parents and children who enjoy bathtime and want to enrich their time together. The activities will introduce children to scientific ideas about air and water. The word "science" might sound ominous, but the activities really don't require any special knowledge or expertise. In fact, they can be just as much fun as splashing and playing in the tub. I hope this book increases bathtime fun for both you and your children.

James Lewis

Acknowledgments

I am grateful to many people who have supported my efforts with this book. Special thanks go to Bruce Lansky, publisher of Meadowbrook Press, for his acceptance of and confidence in the idea for this book. Thanks go to my family for giving me the time to write and for their willingness to sacrifice their needs to support mine. Steve and Cyndy Dustrude kept new materials for this book coming my way. Dick Lennox gave his time and expertise regarding computers and illustrations. Paul Halupa gave me encouragement and the title for this book. Harry Hom pushed me to submit samples of my draft rather than wait longer. Joanne Halgren helped with interlibrary loans. Supporters like Cathy Feier, Sue Thomas, and John Halgren always showed interest. And, finally, thanks go to my mother, who encouraged me to write and publish, a lifelong dream of hers.

J.L.

Making Bathtime Safe

Bathtime can be fun, but it should be safe, too. Follow these simple safety rules to make the bathtub a safe place:

1. **Always check the water temperature before your child gets in.** Remember that the temperature might feel lukewarm to your hand but much hotter to your child's body.

2. **Never leave a young child unattended in the bathtub.** Instead, collect materials for activities prior to bathtime.

3. **Try to use a rubber bathmat in the tub.** These mats help prevent falls when your child gets in and out of the tub. A cloth bathmat outside the tub is equally important.

4. **Help your child get in and out of the bathtub.** Climbing in or out of the tub, even with bathmats, is a likely time for accidents.

5. **Remind your child to sit down in the tub at all times.** Kneeling or standing is risky.

6. **Don't give your child anything to play with that is sharp, breakable, or small and easily swallowed.** Plastic containers work well, but watch out for any with sharp edges. Don't allow dangerous metal or glass in the tub. And, for your own sake, beware of anything small enough to go down the drain!

7. **Clean the materials thoroughly before using them in the activities.** Make sure you remove residues inside plastic containers. Don't use containers that have been used to hold medicines or cleaners.

8. **Make sure that the bathtub rules are clear and that your child understands them.** You'll need to stress and review important ideas such as staying seated, keeping the water in the tub, and cleaning up at the end of bathtime.

A Note to Parents

1. We divided the activities in this book into different age levels. Activities for younger children are more concrete and observable while those for older children tend to be more abstract. However, the age levels are only approximate. *You're* the best judge of what your child can and cannot do.

2. Even if your child is older, you might want to go back to the younger age levels just to make sure he or she understands both the activities and the concepts behind them. For some children, this review builds confidence and helps maintain their interest.

3. I've listed the materials required on the page for each activity, as well as on a master list at the beginning of the book. Most of them are things you already have around the house, and all of them are inexpensive.

4. Don't worry if you don't know the outcome of each activity in advance. You might find that you can learn from these activities, too!

5. Always encourage your child to explain what happens in each activity, but don't require answers or turn the activity into a drill. Let your child enjoy them!

6. Allow your child to repeat the activities. One brief exposure to a new idea might not satisfy a child's natural curiosity.

7. Try doing an activity for more than one bathtime. You might want to use one activity throughout a week, either repeating it or changing it in various ways.

8. The procedures for each activity are only suggestions. Feel free to alter them! You might wish to read the directions first and then rephrase them for your child.

9. Each activity is designed to take only one to five minutes, leaving plenty of time for the child to either repeat it or play with something else.

Materials

Kitchen Supplies:

Aluminum foil
Baster (clear plastic)
Cap (from plastic bottle)
Coffee filter (may substitute cotton cloth)
Cups (paper or plastic)
Food coloring
Funnels (clear plastic are best; 2 small, 2 medium, 2 large)
Ice cubes
Knife
Measuring cups, spoons, and container (plastic)
Milk cartons (plastic and cardboard in three sizes)
Milk jug (plastic, gallon or 4-liter)
Pitchers (plastic, with handle and lip; 2 sizes preferred)
Plastic containers (clear; both wide-mouthed and narrow-necked; stacking and nonstacking)
Plastic spray bottle
Plates (plastic)
Popsicle sticks or tongue depressors
Sandwich or vegetable bags (plastic)
Saucer or flat dish
Sieve
Soft drink bottles with caps (plastic)
Spoons (6 metal)
Straws (clear plastic are best)
Waxed paper
Twist-tie

Household Supplies:

Cardboard (thin, flat)
Comb (plastic)
Corks (different sizes)
Eyedropper (plastic)
Hand pump from squirt bottle
Handkerchief
Marking pen (nontoxic; optional)
Paper (notebook sheets)
Paper towels (sturdy)
Pencil
Plastic tubing (clear, flexible, 3 feet or 1 meter long)
Plastic tube (stiff, clear; 6 inches by ½ inch or 16 centimeters by 1 centimeter)
Rubber bands
Ruler (plastic or wood)
Scissors
Soap (liquid)
String (cotton)
Tape (plastic, duct, or electrical)
Washcloths
Wool cloth (optional)
Yardstick (or meterstick) or stick long enough to reach across the tub

Toys:

Bubble solution and two wands (metal wands work best)
Building blocks (wooden or plastic, about 1 inch or 2.5 centimeters square)
Plasticine (waterproof) clay
Squirt gun
Tub toys (floating and sinkable)
Watercolor paintbrush

Basic
Activities

The Unsinkables

Parent's Note:

Kids see things float—big or small, short or tall, heavy or light. As adults we don't stop to consider how a large ocean liner weighing tons can float as well as a bird's feather. So help your child think about why things float (even if it *is* hard to explain).

What You Need:

A wooden building block; a plastic cap from a soft drink bottle.

What To Do:

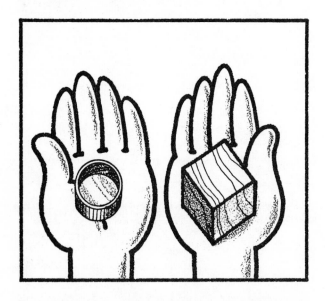

1. All sorts of things float. Try holding a block in one hand and a plastic cap in your other hand. Which feels heavier, the block or the cap?

2. Which one do you think will float? Which one will sink? Put them in the water to find out.

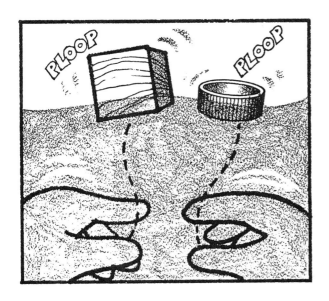

3. Now try pushing them both under the water and letting go. What happens?

4. Let's try some other toys that are heavy and light. Push them under the water. Why do some heavy things float just like the light things do?

What Did You See?

The heavy building block floated just like the light plastic cap. You saw that heavy things can float just as light things do.

Why Did It Happen?

Things float on water if they weigh less than the water. Even though the wood is heavier than the plastic cap, the wood is still lighter than the water directly beneath it.

Shipshape!

Parent's Note:

By now your children are capable of creating variations on an idea. Remember to pose questions and let your children seek the answers. And if they aren't sure of an answer, encourage them to experiment anyway. It's OK for you not to have the answers either. In fact, you might want to experiment yourself. Go ahead! That's great! This one activity can keep you all busy for many days because it has so many possible solutions.

What You Need:

Plasticine clay; aluminum foil; wooden building blocks.

What To Do:

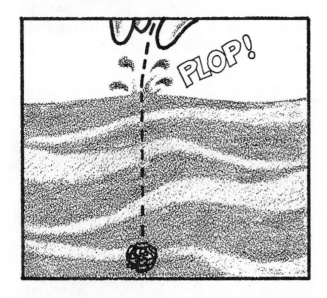

1. You already know about things that either float or sink. Now let's think of something that can both float and sink. Any ideas? Try taking some aluminum foil and squeezing it into a ball. Now drop it in the water. Does it sink or float?

2. Now try straightening the foil and shaping it into a little boat. Does it float now?

3. Now let's do the same thing with some clay. Make a ball first and drop it in the water. Klunk! Now shape the clay into a boat. Does it float now?

4. Let's use both the foil and the clay to make boats that can carry things like wooden blocks. Try to shape the boats so they don't sink or turn over. What shape carries the most blocks?

What Did You See?

You could make foil or clay either sink or float simply by changing its shape.

Why Did It Happen?

The clay and foil balls sink because they are squeezed into small shapes and only a small amount of water is trying to hold up the weight. When you spread out the clay or foil, it floats because the weight is now supported by a lot more water. Think about a big ship on the ocean. If all the materials it takes to build a ship were stacked on the water, they would sink. But when those materials are spread over the water in the shape of a boat, they float.

Building a Raft

Parent's Note:

When your children are finished experimenting with shapes and sizes of foil and clay in the activity "Shipshape," ask them how they can make a ball of clay float with some sticks! Then, without letting them peek at the solutions on this page, give them a round ball of clay and some popsicle sticks and let them have a go at it.

What You Need:

Plasticine clay; popsicle sticks or tongue depressors; a plastic cup; tape.

What To Do:

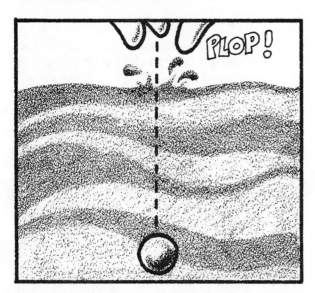

1. Let's try floating a ball of clay again. Does it still sink to the bottom?

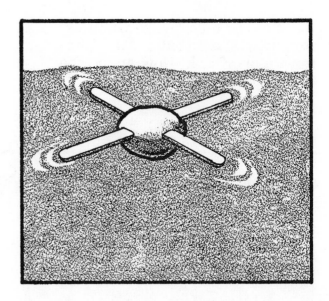

2. Try sticking 2 or 3 popsicle sticks into the clay ball like the rays of the sun. Does that make a difference? Use more sticks. Now will it float?

3. Try floating a plastic cup in the water. Now fill the cup with water. Does it still float?

4. Take two of the sticks and tape them together to make an X. Float the X in the water and set the cup of water on it. Does the cup float now?

What Did You See?

The clay ball sank just like a rock. But when you put sticks in the side like the rays of the sun, the clay ball floated on top of the water. The plastic cup sank when you poured water into it, but floated when you set it on the little raft you made out of sticks.

Why Did It Happen?

The sticks weigh less than the water in the space they take up, so they float; they also help spread the weight of the clay and the cup over a bigger area.

Measuring Up

Parent's Note:

Schools seldom require children to learn the mathematics of volume until the second or third grade; however, if your children help in the kitchen from time to time, they're already aware of the different measuring tools you use. So rather than formally teaching your children that 2 pints equal a quart (or that two ½-liters equal a liter), just provide the containers and let them experiment with measuring volume.

What You Need:

Plastic spoons and cups of different sizes; plastic or cardboard milk containers of different sizes, for example, pint, quart, and gallon (or ½-liter, liter, and 4-liter), several of each size; funnel(s).

What To Do:

1. Let's have fun filling and emptying some containers. We'll start by filling small (pint or ½ liter) containers and then pouring the water through the funnel into a large (quart or liter) container. How many small containers does it take to fill the large container?

2. How many tablespoons will fill a cup? How many cups will fill a quart (liter)?

3. This is a big container—it holds a gallon (or 4 liters) of water! How many of these quart (or liter) containers does it take to fill the gallon (or 4-liter) container? Try guessing before you fill it. Were you right?

4. Now fill the gallon (or 4-liter) container and then pour water into little containers. How many pint (or ½-liter) containers does it fill? How many cups?

What Did You See?

Water in containers could be poured into other containers. You could put more water in big containers than in little ones. The same size containers always held the same amount of water.

Why Did It Happen?

Water takes the shape of whatever container it's in. It can also fit in any size container. We give names to containers of certain sizes, such as a quart (or liter). That way, any time we fill up one of those containers we know just how much water (or any other liquid) we have.

Let's Swing

Parent's Note:

Children love to play on swings—they never seem to get enough of it. This activity helps explain how swings work. You'll need to help with this one, unless you can find a suitable place to hang the bottle so it swings above your bathtub. Good luck!

What You Need:

A string about 1 foot (or 1/3 meter) long; a clear plastic bottle large enough to hold a quart (or liter) of water.

What To Do:

1. Let's make a water swing! First, we'll tie a string around the neck of a plastic bottle. Now Mom or Dad will hold the string so you can push the bottle while you're sitting in the tub. Push! See it swing! How many times does it swing back and forth?

2. Now let's fill the bottle about half-way full with water. Start it swinging again. Now let's count! Does it swing the same number of times? More? Not as many?

3. Fill the bottle to the brim, swing it, and count again!

4. Now twist the empty bottle a few times, let go, and watch it spin! Fill it with water and try again. Does the bottle spin longer with water or without water?

What Did You See?

When the bottle had water in it, it swung and spun longer than when it was empty.

Why Did It Happen?

Water has weight, so once it starts moving in one direction it keeps going that way! This is called "inertia." When you are running one way and want to go back the other way, it takes you a little time to slow down, turn around, and start back the other way. The same thing happens on a swing when you stop pumping—you still keep going for a long time! And, just like a swing, the bottle goes back and forth more times when it has weight in it than when it's empty.

The Sprinkler

Parent's Note:

Now that you're in the swing of things, try one more swinging activity with your child. This time the container will shoot out water as it turns, like a sprinkler, so make sure you hold it over the tub. Also make sure that each of the holes you make is slanting at the same angle; if not, the container will not spin properly. Good Luck!

What You Need:

A piece of string about 2 feet (or ⅔ meter) long; a rectangular milk carton with the top intact.

What To Do:

1. Let's make a water sprinkler for the tub! First Mom or Dad will put one hole in the lower left corner of each side of a milk carton. Be sure all four holes are slanting in the same direction. Then, attach a string to the thick ridge at the top of the carton and cut a hole in the top.

2. Now Mom or Dad will hold it over the tub and pour water into the top of the carton. Wow! Watch it sprinkle and spin!

3. Now Mom or Dad will put more holes in the container.

4. What happens when you pour in water now? Does the carton spin slower or faster?

What Did You See?

When you filled the milk carton with water, the water squirted out the holes in one direction and pushed the milk carton in the opposite direction, spinning it in a circle. When you added more holes, more water squirted out and the carton spun faster.

Why Did It Happen?

The weight of the water in the milk carton pushes the water out the holes near the bottom. The force of the water squirting out the holes pushes the milk carton and it starts to spin because the water is spraying from holes that are all pointed the same way.

Pump It Up

Parent's Note:

A little preparation for this activity helps. First you'll need to collect different types of toy and household pumps. Then do your best to direct the pump spray into the tub! I haven't tried to explain in this activity *why* the pump works the way it does. Instead, this activity will pique your children's curiosity so they'll be ready to learn the principles later.

What You Need:

Various pumps such as a squirt gun, a pump sprayer, a plastic eyedropper, and a baster.

What To Do:

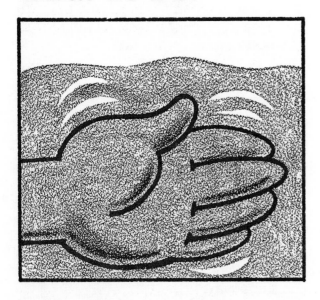

1. We know that water moves when you push it, dip it, or pour it. Use your hands to move the water around the tub. Now try pouring it. Good! Another way to move water is to *pump* it.

2. We can use an eyedropper and baster. Try sucking water up into the tube and then squirting it back out!

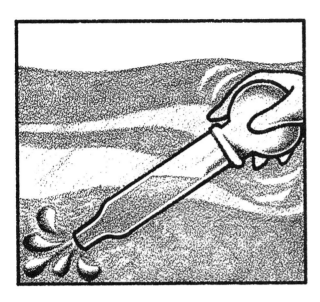

3. Now suck up some more water and try squirting it back out *under* the water. What happens?

4. Two other kinds of pumps are the ones that come on sprayers and in squirt guns. Try squirting these pumps in and out of the water. What is the same about these and the eyedropper and the baster?

What Did You See?

When you squeezed the pump in the water, you made bubbles. When you stopped squeezing, the pump filled up with water. Squeezing the pump when it was full of water made the water squirt out.

Why Did It Happen?

A pump sucks water up inside a tube. Squeezing the bulb or trigger under water pushes air out of the tube, which makes bubbles, and releasing the bulb or trigger lets the water come in. When you squeeze the bulb or trigger again, it pushes the *water* out and lets either air or water back in.

The Magic Straw

Parent's Note:

Dipping water with a straw, which works much the same way a pump does, is a real mystery for most kids. It's also a trick that you may wish your kids had never discovered—especially in restaurants! But straw dipping *is* another good way of moving water from one place to another. In fact, this technique is used by lab technicians and scientists every day.

What You Need:

A container; straws—clear are the best.

What To Do:

1. Let's see if we can use a straw to move water from the tub into this container. First try dropping the straw in the water. Now plug both ends with your fingers and empty the water into the container. Does that work? Can you think of any other ways? Try them!

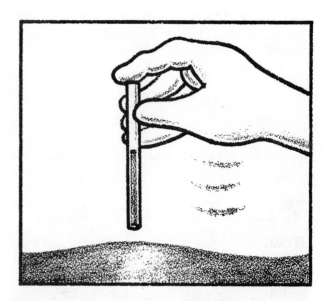

2. Now try putting the straw in the water and closing only one end with your finger. Keep your finger there and lift the straw out of the water. What happens to the water in the straw?

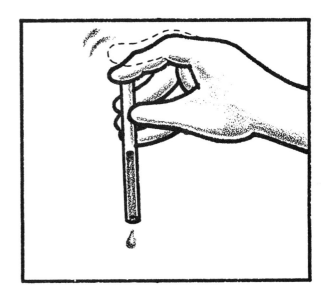

3. Now hold the straw over the container with your finger still over the end. What happens when you take your finger off the end of the straw?

4. Practice taking your finger off the end of the straw and then quickly putting it back on. What happens to the flow of water?

What Did You See?

The straw held the water inside as long as your finger was over the end. When you took your finger off, the water drained out. Each time you let go, small amounts of water dripped out until you quickly covered the straw again.

Why Did It Happen?

Air presses on everything, even on the water in the straw. We call this *air pressure*. Air presses from every direction. When you put your finger over the straw, you trap the air in the straw. When you lift the straw out of the water, a few drops fall out, leaving extra room for the air. Since the trapped air has more room to move around, it doesn't press on the water in the straw as hard. The air outside the straw still presses up against the water just as hard as ever. Now the air pressure outside is greater than the air pressure inside of the straw, so it keeps the water in the straw.

The Lidless Bottle

Parent's Note:

How can we put water in a bottle without a cap, turn the bottle upside down, and *not* have the water spill out? This activity will help you explain this riddle to your child.

What You Need:

Several narrow-necked, clear plastic bottles or other containers.

What To Do:

1. Let's fill a bottle with water and then turn it over above the tub. What happens? Splash!

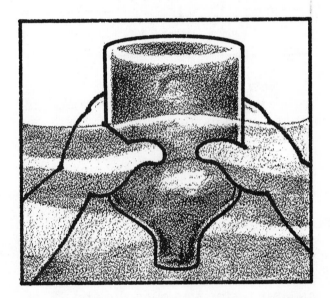

2. Let's fill the bottle again and hold it under the water. Now, slowly turn the bottle so the small open end is facing down—still under the water—and the large end is pointed up out of the water. Is any of the water in the bottle higher than the water in the tub?

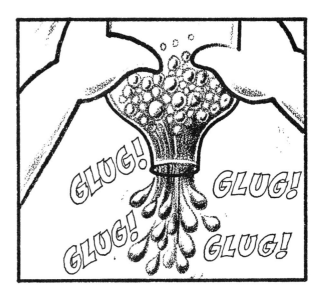

3. Slowly lift the bottle up so the small end is barely in the water. Is the water still in the bottle? How could that happen?

4. Now lift the bottle completely out of the water. What happens?

What Did You See?

When you held the full bottle upside down above the water, all the water in it drained out. But when you turned it upside down under the water, the water stayed in—until you lifted it completely out of the water again.

Why Did It Happen?

Air doesn't seem very heavy, but it does have weight. Air presses down on everything, even the water in the tub. When the air presses down, the water in the tub pushes back up into the bottle and keeps the water in the bottle from falling out. Even if you had a bottle as tall as the ceiling, air pressure would keep the water in it from draining out!

Upside-Down Magic

What You Need:

A wide-mouthed, clear plastic container; thin cardboard big enough to cover the mouth of the container.

What To Do:

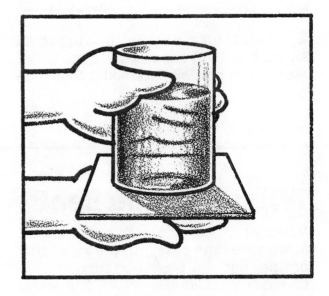

1. Do you want to see what other tricks air pressure can do? Let's fill a container with water almost to the top and then put a piece of cardboard over the mouth.

2. Put your hand firmly on the cardboard, turn the container over quickly, and hold it steady. Got it?

3. Now let go of the cardboard. Can you believe it? It doesn't fall off!

4. Try it again! What happens when you use more water? Less water? Have fun with your new magic trick!

What Did You See?

The cardboard stayed in place and the water stayed in the container even though you turned the container upside down!

Why Did It Happen?

There's more air outside the container than inside it, so there is more air *pressure* outside than inside. The outside air pressure pushes the cardboard onto the mouth of the container even when it's upside down!

Dry-Paper Mystery

Parent's Note:

Kids love riddles and mysteries. Try this one out on your child: "How can you keep a piece of paper dry when it's all the way under the water?" Then get ready to show how it's done! You can do this experiment in a bathtub, a sink, or even a bucket of water.

What You Need:

A clear plastic container; a piece of notebook paper.

What To Do:

1. First, crumple up a piece of paper and shove it all the way down to the bottom of the container. Make sure the paper doesn't fall out when you turn the container over.

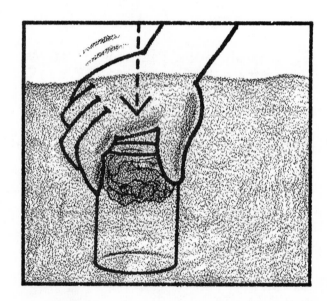

2. Now turn the container upside down and push it all the way under the water. Keep it straight!

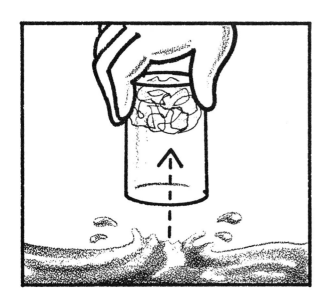

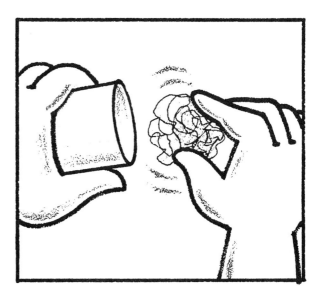

3. Now lift the container out of the water. Don't turn it over until it's all the way out!

4. Take the paper out of the container. Look! It's dry!

What Did You See?

Did you think the paper might get all wet and mushy? Well, it didn't, did it? It stayed nice and dry.

Why Did It Happen?

The container was full of air when you put it in the water. By putting it in upside down, you kept the air from getting out, so there was no room for the water to get in and wet the paper.

Push and Pull

Parent's Note:

Kids—and some adults—often take the properties of water for granted and don't stop to think why some simple things happen. For instance, why does combing your hair with water help hold it in place? Why does your hair stick to your head when you get out of the shower or swimming pool? And why does a paintbrush form a point when dipped in water?

What You Need:

A paintbrush; waxed paper; a clear plastic container.

What To Do:

1. Let's see how close you can get 2 drops of water before they join together. Using a paintbrush, put 2 drops of water on a sheet of waxed paper and try moving them closer to each other with the brush. What happens when the drops touch each other?

2. Now try to separate the 2 drops again. Is it harder to put drops together or pull them apart? Try taking 1 drop and brushing it around with the paintbrush.

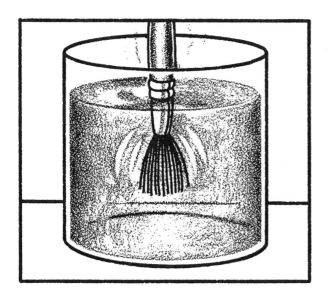

3. Now let's put the brush in water and see what happens to the hairs! Does the water push the hairs apart or pull them together?

4. What happens when you pull the brush out of the water? Surprised?

What Did You See?

You saw those water drops on the waxed paper get closer and closer, and when they got very, very close, they joined together! Try as you might, you couldn't get them apart. And when you pushed the dry paintbrush into the water, the hairs spread apart. But snap!—they pulled together again when you lifted the brush out of the water.

Why Did It Happen?

Water drops like to stick together. That's why your hair sticks together when you put water on it and your swimming suit sticks to you when you go swimming.

Stick with Me!

Parent's Note:

Remember times when you've stacked 1 glass inside another and then couldn't pull them apart? If they were wet, they seemed to stick together even more. If the containers for this activity were glass they would stick together even better, but remember, no glass in the tub! Using plastic containers will at least give your child a feel for the "strength" of water, the binding force between its molecules.

What You Need:

2 plastic, stackable containers; 2 sheets of paper; 2 plastic plates.

What To Do:

1. Sometimes when we stack containers inside each other they stick together. Put 1 plastic container firmly inside the other and then pull them apart. Remember to keep them dry! Is it easy or hard to do?

2. This time let's get the containers wet and then stack them together again. We can dump any extra water out.

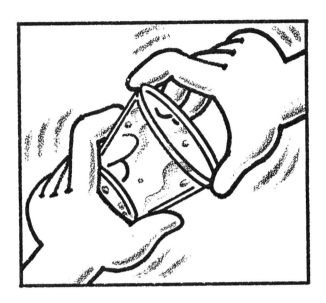

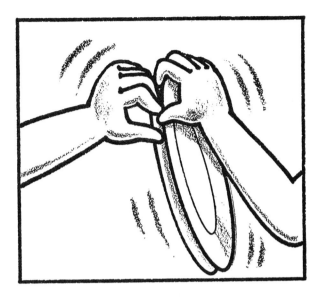

3. Now try to pull them apart. Is it easier to pull them apart when they are wet or dry?

4. Now try taking 2 sheets of paper apart when they're dry and again when they're wet. You can also try some plates or pieces of plastic.

What Did You See?

The containers came apart more easily when they were dry than when they were wet.

Why Did It Happen?

Tiny drops of water cling tightly to each other. When you try to pull the wet containers apart, you are trying to pull the water apart, too. If you could see the water *very* closely, it would look like glue stretching between your fingers!

How Strong Is Water?

Parent's Note:

Once again, you'll need a little time and ingenuity to gather materials and set up this activity, but it's well worth the effort. Your child will see just how strong water molecules are, and just how much force you have to apply to break the bond between them.

What You Need:

A yardstick (or meterstick) that stretches from one side of the tub to the other; a plastic or wooden ruler; string; a paper cup; cardboard; a pitcher.

What To Do:

1. We'll need Mom or Dad's help with this. We're going to make a scale in the tub! First, let's place a stick across the tub.

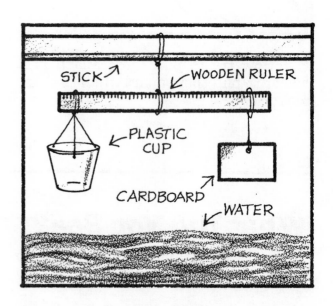

STICK
WOODEN RULER
PLASTIC CUP
CARDBOARD
WATER

2. A ruler will be the scale. Use string and tape to attach a cup to one end of the ruler and a flat cardboard square to the other end. Now take a string and tie one end to the middle of the stick and the other end to the middle of the ruler. Balance the ruler so the 2 ends are the same distance from the water.

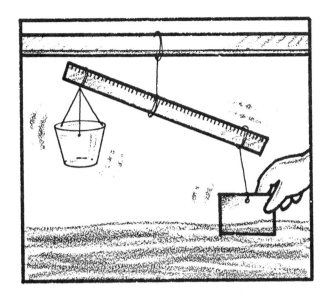

3. Next, let's tip the cardboard down to the water. What happens? Does it stay down on the water? Yes! The water acts like glue.

4. Now pour some water into the cup. How much water will we need to pour into the cup to pull the cardboard off the water?

What Did You See?

The water grabbed the cardboard and wouldn't let go until you put a lot of water in the cup.

Why Did It Happen?

The tiny drops of water cling tightly to each other! The water drops holding the cardboard were *so* strong that it took all the weight of the water in the cup to break their grip.

Magic Comb

You've been to parties where you rub a balloon on your hair and then stick it to the wall or ceiling. Water, like a balloon, reacts to static electrical charges coming from a comb or plastic spoon. The water stream has to be very small, though, and your child's hair must be dry for this activity to work. If your child's hair doesn't charge the comb or spoon, use something made of wool.

What You Need:

A comb; a plastic spoon; wool cloth (optional).

What To Do:

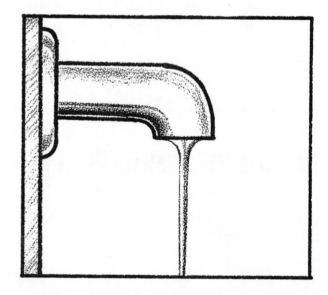

1. When you comb your hair, does it ever make popping sounds or stand up a little? It does this because of something called "static electricity." Comb your hair now to see if you can make some static electricity! (The comb must be dry; a wet one won't take a charge.)

2. Let's see if this static electricity can make water move, too. First, turn on the tub water so it flows in a *very* small stream.

3. Quickly run a *dry* comb through your *dry* hair and then hold the comb near—but not in—the stream of water. Now look from the side. What happens to the water?

4. Let's try it again! This time rub a plastic spoon in your hair and then hold it near the water. Or try using some wool cloth to charge a comb or a spoon. What works best?

What Did You See?

The water moved toward the charged comb or spoon.

Why Did It Happen?

The water drops are attracted to the electrical charge in the comb just like your hair is attracted to the charge in the comb. Actually, the water drops are stretching toward the electrical charge in the comb because they are attracted to electricity.

Disappearing Act

Parent's Note:

This activity might take as long as a week to complete, so be patient. Try to find a quiet corner where you can keep a single container—undisturbed—for a week. Put up a big sign: "Please do not disturb!"

What You Need:

A tall, thin, wide-mouthed, clear plastic container; a marking pen or tape.

What To Do:

1. How would you like to make water disappear without touching it? Let's fill a container almost to the top. Next we'll use tape or a marker to mark how high the water comes up on the side.

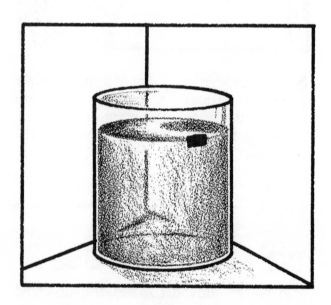

2. Now let's set the container in a corner where it won't be disturbed. Don't cover it with anything!

3. Each day take a look to see how much water is left.

4. After a week, mark on the container where the water level is. How much water is there compared to how much you put in?

What Did You See?

After one week the water level was far below where it was when you filled it!

Why Did It Happen?

Water jumps into the air when air touches it. We call this process *evaporation*. Water evaporates faster in a warm room than in a cold room. You can't see the water that has evaporated, but you know that it must have gone into the air because it's no longer in the container!

Hang It Up

Parent's Note:

Here's another evaporation activity. You'll like this one—it reinforces the idea of hanging towels on the rack to dry rather than leaving them wadded up on the floor!

What You Need:

3 washcloths; 2 clear plastic sandwich or vegetable bags; a rubber band or a plastic twist-tie.

What To Do:

1. Let's try some different ways of drying out a wet washcloth and see which works best. First, let's get a washcloth wet, wring it out, and put it in a plastic bag. Then we'll tie the bag shut nice and tight!

2. Now let's get a second washcloth wet, wring it out, and put it in another plastic bag. This time we'll leave the top *open*. We can put this bag and the other one on the corner of the tub.

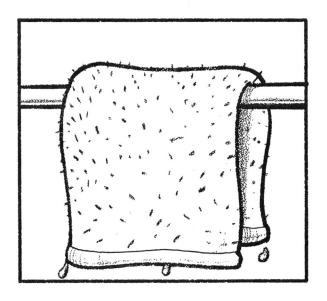

3. Let's get the last washcloth wet, wring it out, open it, and hang it on the towel rack.

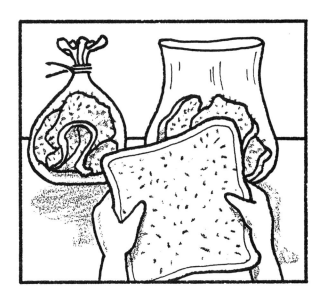

4. Check each washcloth tomorrow before your bath. Which one dried the fastest? Why?

What Did You See?

The next day you found that the washcloth in the tied plastic bag was still just as wet as when you put it in. The washcloth in the open plastic bag was still wet in places. But the washcloth spread out on the towel rack was completely dry!

Why Did It Happen?

Wet things dry the fastest when all the wet parts are open to the air. Wet things that aren't stretched out still have places in the folds and creases that the air hasn't reached yet. Towels left wadded up on the floor don't dry out quickly and usually aren't dry the next time you want to use them. And we know how nice dry towels are for drying you off!

Was I That Dirty?

Parent's Note:

Save this activity until your kids have been playing in the dirt and are good and filthy. Before they climb into the tub, have them look at and think about the clean water. At the end of the bathtime, you'll get a chance to filter the dirt from some of the bathwater. This activity will reaffirm what you already know as the most predictable outcome of bathtime: ring around the tub!

What You Need:

A coffee filter or a sheer, clean, white cotton cloth; some sort of sieve to hold the filter or cloth; a pitcher.

What To Do:

1. Before you get in the tub, take a look at the water. Where did it come from? Was it always so clear and clean?

2. Now that your bathtime is almost finished, look at the water in the tub. Is it as clear and clean as when you started? Why not?

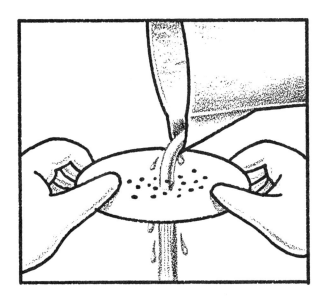

3. Fill a pitcher with some of the water from your bath. Let Mom or Dad hold a filter while you pour the bathwater through it. What do you see in the filter?

4. Now let's put the filter over the drain of the tub and drain the water. Wait until a lot of water has gone down and then check the filter. What do you see now? Can you believe you were *that* dirty?

What Did You See?

The water was clean and clear at the beginning of the bath, but not at the end. When you poured the tub water through the filter, some small pieces of dirt were caught in the filter. Some dirt was also left around the tub and on the bottom. The filter over the drain collected even more dirt from the water.

Why Did It Happen?

Water gets between dirt and your skin and loosens the dirt. Then the dirt drops off you and either floats in the water or falls to the bottom. The filter catches pieces of dirt as the water flows through it, so it helps clean the water. Most of the dirt in the tub is *so* small that it goes right through the filter. You'd need a very special filter to get your bathwater clean enough to use again!

Mystery Ice

What You Need:

A wide-mouthed, clear plastic container; a marking pen or tape; ice cubes; a saucer or dish to catch the overflow.

What To Do:

1. What happens when you put ice cubes in a glass of water? Let's find out. First, fill the container half full and mark the water level. Dry your hands and drop in the ice cubes. Where is the water level now? Mark it.

2. Now leave the ice cubes in the container until they melt. Guess where the water level will be! Where you right?

3. Now fill the container to the top so that it's brimming but not overflowing. Dry your hands and drop the ice cubes into the water. What happens?

4. Let's try it again, but this time let's put the ice cubes in *before* we fill the container to the top. Wait until the ice cubes melt. What happens to the water level? Surprised?

What Did You See?

When you dropped the ice cubes into the container of water, the water either rose or spilled out. When the ice cubes melted, the water level didn't change!

Why Did It Happen?

Water does a strange thing when it freezes—it gets bigger! When water is frozen into an ice cube, it acts like a block of wood by taking up space and pushing the water out. However, when it melts, it gets smaller again, and the water level goes back down.

Advanced Activities

What's Inside?

Parent's Note:

We've already looked at some ways to make a clay ball sink or float. One method was to reshape clay so it displaced more water. Another way was to place popsicle sticks or straws into the clay to give it added contact with the water. This activity will add another method. And maybe, between you and your child, you'll think of others!

What You Need:

Plasticine clay; a piece of wood that is either round or square, but only ½ inch (or 1.3 centimeters) in diameter.

What To Do:

1. What will a clay ball do when you drop it in the water? How do you know? Try it! How about a piece of wood? Does it sink or float?

2. How could you use the wood to make the clay ball float? Any ideas? Try setting the clay ball on top of the block. Does the clay float? Why not?

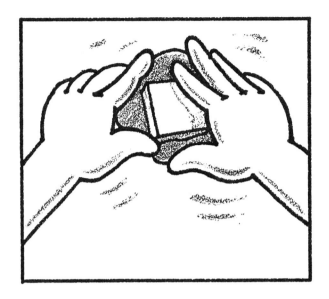

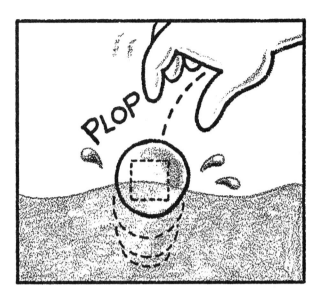

3. Now try putting the wood *inside* the clay ball. Shape the clay so it's still in the shape of a ball.

4. What happens when you put the clay in the water now? It floats! Could you fool someone if you had 2 clay balls, one with wood in the middle and one without?

What Did You See?

The clay ball sank to the bottom of the tub. But when you put the wood inside the clay, it floated!

Why Did It Happen?

The wooden block inside the clay was lighter than water, so it helped to hold up the heavy clay ball. Even though the same amount of clay was used, the piece of wood made the size of the ball bigger, spreading the weight of the clay over more water, which made it float.

Weigh It

What You Need:

String; 6 metal soup spoons all the same size and shape; a ruler; tape.

What To Do:

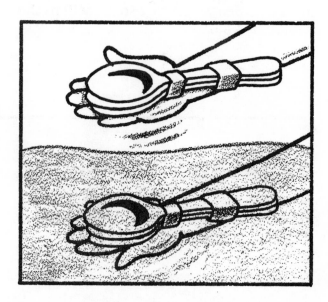

1. Tape together 3 spoons. Hold them in your hand. How do they feel—heavy or light? Now drop them in the water. What happens?

2. Tape 3 more spoons together. Hold a set of spoons in each hand. Lower one hand into the water and keep the other hand out of the water. Which spoons feel heavier—those in the water or those out?

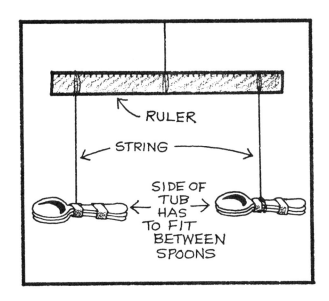

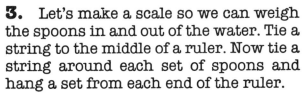

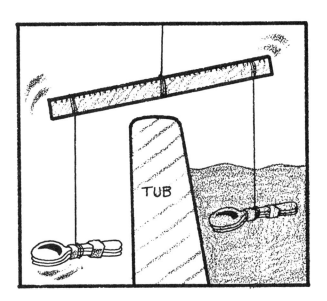

3. Let's make a scale so we can weigh the spoons in and out of the water. Tie a string to the middle of a ruler. Now tie a string around each set of spoons and hang a set from each end of the ruler.

4. Hold the ruler up by the middle string and balance the scale so it is even. Now lower it over the edge of the tub so one set of spoons hangs in the water and the other set hangs outside the edge of the tub. What happens to the scale? Which set of spoons is lighter? Which is heavier?

What Did You See?

The spoons were not as heavy in the water.

Why Did It Happen?

When any object is placed in water, it weighs less. Even when something is too heavy to float, the water still helps support its weight. That's why it's easy for your mom or dad to give you a piggyback ride in the swimming pool—you weigh a lot less in the water than you do on dry land.

On the Level

Parent's Note:

Besides teaching about the curious or fun aspects of air and water, bathtime can also teach children about tools that use water and air. Some children at this age have seen a carpenter's level, and a few might already understand why it's so useful. In this activity you can help your child make one and then put it to use. Is the tub level? The floor?

What You Need:

Plasticine clay; a straight, rigid, clear plastic tube about 6 inches (or 15 centimeters) long; flat cardboard; waxed paper; tape.

What To Do:

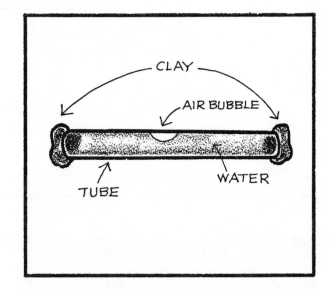

1. Let's put waxed paper over a piece of cardboard and put a drop of water on the middle. Now try to hold the cardboard so that the drop doesn't roll off. What happens if you tilt the cardboard? How can you keep the water drop in the middle?

2. We're going to build a *level*. It will tell us whether a surface is flat or tilted. First, plug one end of a tube with clay, fill it almost full of water, and then plug the other end.

46

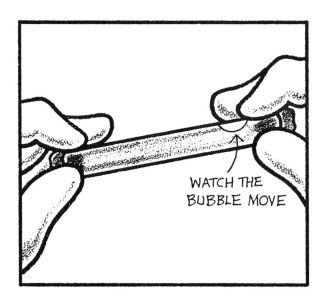

WATCH THE BUBBLE MOVE

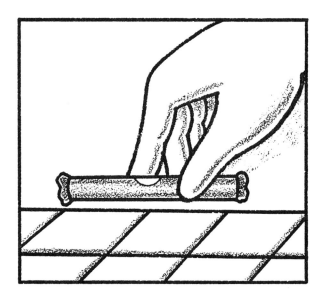

3. Can you see an air bubble inside the tube? What happens to the bubble when you tilt the tube? What happens to the bubble when you hold the tube level?

4. Can you think of a way to use the level? Try laying it on the bottom of the tub. Now lay it on the side of the tub. How can you tell when a surface is level?

What Did You See?

The air bubble moved when you tilted the level, but it stayed in the middle when you kept the level very flat.

Why Did It Happen?

The bubble stays in the middle when the tube is perfectly level—that's why it's called a level! If you tilt the tube even a little bit, all the water (which is heavy) moves to the low end of the tube, and the air bubble (which is light) rises to the high end. Carpenters use a level like this to make sure each board, wall, door, and window is perfectly straight.

All Stopped Up

Your child has seen how powerful air can be. It was strong enough to displace water in "On the Level." In this activity the air in a bottle is so strong that it can stop water even when the water has help from a funnel.

What You Need:

Plasticine clay; a narrow-necked, clear plastic container; a funnel that will fit easily into the neck of the container; a pitcher or cup.

What To Do:

1. Sometimes air is strong enough to push water out of the way. Let's see if air can stop water that is coming through a funnel. Start by placing a funnel in the top of a bottle.

2. Now pour water into the bottle through the funnel. What happened? The bottle filled right up! Now let's pour the water out of the bottle.

3. Next, let's seal the funnel in the bottle with some clay so that no air can get in or out except through the funnel.

4. Now pour water in the funnel again. What happened this time?

What Did You See?

The water you poured into the unsealed funnel filled it to the top and overflowed. The water you poured into the sealed funnel flowed into the bottle a little and then stopped. The rest of the water in the funnel would not flow into the bottle.

Why Did It Happen?

When the funnel is sealed, the air in the bottle gets trapped between the water that first flowed in and the water in the funnel above. The air stops any more water from coming in until the air can find some way out. When you first turn a faucet back on after the water's been shut off for repairs, you hear the loud sound of air coming out of the faucet. The air that has been trapped in the pipe has to come out before any water can.

Waterwheel Power

Parent's Note:

Your child has already learned some of the ways that water can move things from one place to another. Water can also be used to turn a waterwheel that is especially designed to lift something. You might begin this activity by asking, "How can water lift things?"

What You Need:

Cardboard from a milk carton or shirt box—something with a wax or paint coating to make it water repellent; a straw; string; a pencil; tape; scissors.

What To Do:

1. To make a waterwheel, cut a circle out of some cardboard and make a hole in the center large enough to stick a straw through. Next, cut 4 slits in the circle that point straight toward the center like spokes in a wheel. Don't cut all of the way to the hole in the center.

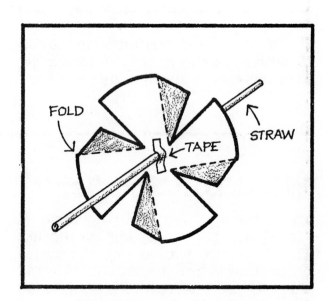

2. Now fold half of each section of the wheel so it sticks out from the rest of the wheel. Next let's put a straw through the hole and tape it to the wheel on both sides.

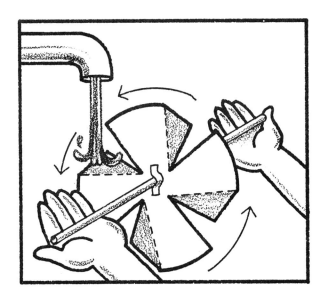

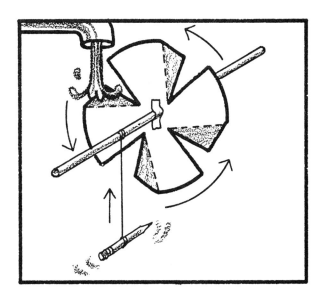

3. Put the waterwheel under a faucet (use a small stream of water at first) and hold the ends of the straw loosely in your hands. The sections of the wheel that stick out will catch the water and make the wheel turn. Look at it go!

4. Let's tape some string to the straw and tie a pencil to the other end of the string. Now we're ready to see if our waterwheel can lift things! Watch the pencil go up.

What Did You See?

When the water struck the waterwheel, the wheel turned. Since the straw was attached to the wheel, it turned, too, and the string wound around the straw, pulling the block up.

Why Did It Happen?

Water has weight and it pushed down on the flat part of the wheel and forced the wheel and the straw to turn. In some factories years ago, there was no electricity. Water turned large waterwheels that turned the other wheels that ground wheat and sawed wood.

Soap-Powered Boat

What You Need:

A thin piece of cardboard or poster board; liquid soap; an eyedropper or straw; scissors.

What To Do:

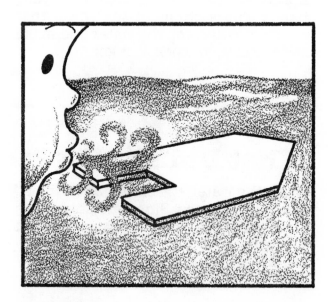

1. Let's make a boat to sail in the tub! Cut a boat out of cardboard in the shape shown above.

2. Put the boat in the water and try to make it go to the far end of the tub without touching it. Try making waves or blowing on it. Is it moving?

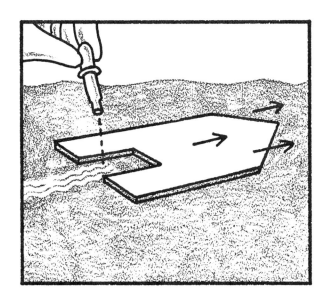

3. Now let's put a drop of soap in the slot at the back. Watch closely! What happens to the boat?

4. Now try putting several drops in the slot. Does the boat move faster or slower? See if you can get the boat to the end of the tub!

What Did You See?

The boat moved forward when you dropped soap in the slot.

Why Did It Happen?

At first, the water drops around the boat were pulling on it the same amount in every direction, so it stayed in one place. Putting the soap in the slot at the rear of the boat weakened the strength of the water behind the boat, so the pull of the water in front was stronger. The water pulled the boat forward just as if there were an invisible thread or rope pulling it!

The Riverboat

Parent's Note:

Another way to make objects move in water—perhaps the most obvious to kids—is the moving propeller. Most boats have motors that turn propellers underwater. For this activity we'll use a special propeller called a paddlewheel. The motor will be a conventional rubber band, any size you like!

What You Need:

Cardboard that is thin, stiff, and flat so you can cut it with a scissors; 2 rubber bands; plastic, electrical, or duct tape; a plastic soft drink bottle with cap; 2 popsicle sticks; scissors.

What To Do:

1. Cut some cardboard into the shape of a boat. Cut another strip (small enough to fit in the back of the boat), tape it to the rubber band, and tape both ends of the rubber band to the boat.

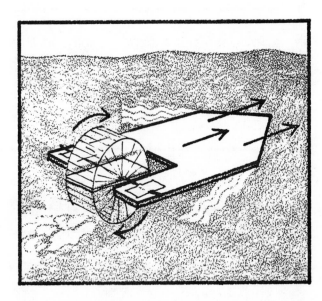

2. This is called a paddlewheel boat. Wind up the paddle on the rubber band. Now put it in the water. Zoom! Can you make the boat go forward *and* backward?

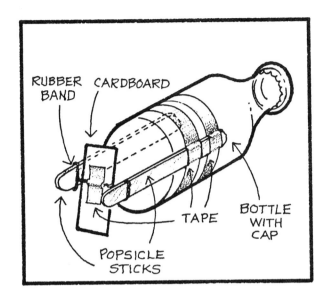

3. Another way to make a paddlewheel boat is to tape 2 popsicle sticks to the side of an empty plastic soft drink bottle tightly capped. Tape a cardboard paddle between the sticks.

4. Wind up the paddle and put it in the water. Watch it go! Can you think of some other ways to make a paddlewheel boat? Try making some boats and having a race.

What Did You See?

When you twisted the paddle and let it go, the boat moved through the water. If you twisted the paddle one way, the boat moved forward. If you twisted the paddle the other way, it went backward.

Why Did It Happen?

The twisted rubber band stores up power. When it unwinds, it uses that power to push the water one way and the boat the other way.

Two-Straw Magic

Parent's Note:

Your child has tried all sorts of ways to move water around in the tub. Well, here's another one! This isn't an easy one, though. You might need a few tries to figure it out, but don't go on to the next activity until you get this one to work. It's fun once it does!

What You Need:

A clear plastic drinking glass or other container; a clear straw; a sturdy paper towel; food coloring; scissors.

What To Do:

1. Remember how eyedroppers and basters suck up water in "Pump It Up"? You can do the same thing with a straw. Let's start by putting a few drops of food coloring in a container nearly filled with water.

2. Now cut a straw in half and put one of the halves in the water. Hold it straight up with your hand!

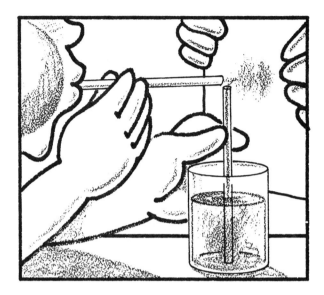

3. Now hold the second half of the straw near the opening of the first half. Mom or Dad will hold a paper towel on the other side of the container. Now blow!

4. Look at the paper towel. Is it changing color? Try tilting the straw a little. Keep blowing until water moves up the straw in the cup and colors the paper towel.

What Did You See?

If you blew just right, water came up the small straw and sprayed onto the paper towel.

Why Did It Happen?

Blowing through the straw causes the air to move very quickly past the end of the straw in the cup, pulling the air out of the straw, and leaving an empty space (vacuum) in its place. Then the room air pushes water up into the straw in the cup to take the air's place. As you keep blowing, you pull some of the *water* out of the straw in the cup and blow it onto the paper towel.

Blow It Up

Parent's Note:

Now that you've caught your breath after the last activity, are you ready for another one? It takes a bit of wind, but it's easier to do than the last one. Just encourage your child to huff and puff away!

What You Need:

A plastic soft drink bottle; a flexible, clear plastic tube about 3 feet (or 1 meter) long.

What To Do:

1. Fill a bottle with water and have Mom or Dad hold it in the water so it stands straight up with the mouth of the bottle pointing to the bottom of the tub. How can you fill this bottle with air without taking it out of the water?

2. A tube can help you fill the bottle with air. Put one end of a tube into the mouth of the bottle and hold the other end up out of the tub.

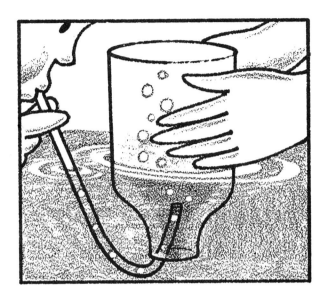

3. Now start blowing into the tube. Watch what happens to the water! It isn't staying in the bottle. Instead, the bottle is filling up with air! Can you blow all of the water out?

4. Test your lungs to see how much air they hold. Fill up the bottle again and put the tube in place. Now take a deep breath and blow once into the tube until you can't blow anymore. The air in the bottle is the amount your lungs can hold.

What Did You See?

As you blew air into the bottle, the air pushed the water out.

Why Did It Happen?

If it has enough force behind it, air can move water. This time, your lungs were so strong they *pushed* the air into the bottle so hard that the air pushed the water right out!

Just Drifting Along

Parent's Note:

Where do things go when they float? That's
the question we'll answer in this activity.
Sometimes the wind blows a floating object
to one end of a wading pool. Sometimes
waves or ocean currents carry driftwood to
the beach. But along with wind, waves, and
currents, there's something else that con-
trols where things float. That something
else is the surface tension created by water
molecules.

What You Need:

A wide-mouthed, clear plastic container;
a pitcher or cup; an eyedropper; a small
cork or plastic bottle cap.

What To Do:

1. Let's fill a container half full of water. Now drop a cork into the water.

2. Without touching the container or
the cork, try to find a way to make the
cork float in the center of the water. Can
you do it? The cork keeps floating to the
side!

3. Now let's try slowly pouring water into the container. Don't pour it on the cork! Keep pouring until the water is to the top of the container.

4. Using the eyedropper, add just a drop of water at a time until the top is bulging with water. What happens? Try pushing the cork to the side with your finger. It comes right back to the middle!

What Did You See?

The cork stayed on one side even when you filled the container to the brim. It was only when you filled the container *over* the brim that the cork moved to the center.

Why Did It Happen?

The cork moved to the middle because the water surface began to curve upward, so the center became the highest point. The cork will always float to the highest possible point, just like it did when the container was only partly full. When the container was partly full, the water curved upward on the *sides* because the water was clinging to the side of the container. Try it again and watch closely from the side, and you *might* be able to see it better!

They're Only Bubbles

Parent's Note:

Boiling water is something you just can't do in the tub! By this age, though, kids know basically what it means to boil water. The water gets very hot and forms bubbles—especially at the bottom of the pan—that rise to the surface. This activity gives the illusion of boiling water because the bubbles come to the top of the container.

What You Need:

A clear, plastic container small enough for your child to grip easily; a handkerchief.

What To Do:

1. Let's see if we can make water boil without heating it! We'll start by filling a clear plastic container almost full. Now let's wet a handkerchief, wring it out, and put it over the top of the container. Smooth it out!

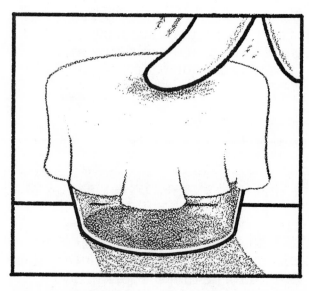

2. Now push the handkerchief downward so that the middle is touching the water. Put your hand over the top and (keeping the container over the tub!) turn it upside down very quickly.

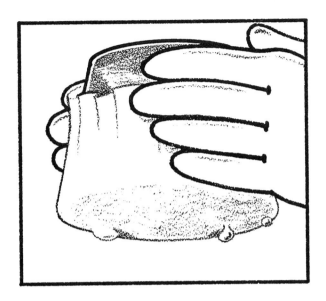

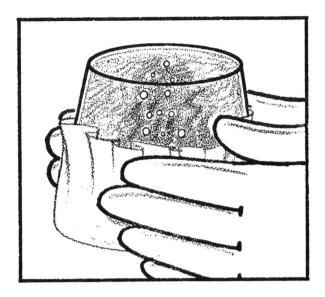

3. Hold the cloth on the sides as best you can with your hand and peek under the container. What do you see?

4. Next, look at the water inside the container and tap on the top. If nothing happens, turn the container just a bit. Do you see bubbles? Is it boiling?

What Did You See?

The water did not come out of the container when you turned it over (at least, not much!). Tapping on the container or turning it made some bubbles come to the surface.

Why Did It Happen?

When you tap or turn the container, the cloth over the mouth of the container stretches tighter and drops down. That makes more room inside the container, so air from the outside rushes in through the tiny holes in the cloth to make air bubbles in the water and fill up the extra space.

Deep-Sea Diver

Parent's Note:

This activity is so simple that your child may even want to use it for show-and-tell! You can use many types of large plastic containers; the secret is to make sure the top fits tightly. Another trick is to test the eyedropper first in the tub water to make sure the top barely touches the water surface when it floats.

What You Need:

A plastic eyedropper; a clear plastic soft drink, syrup, or soap bottle with a tight-fitting cap.

What To Do:

1. Let's try to make an eyedropper sink and float without touching it. First, fill a bottle part way with water.

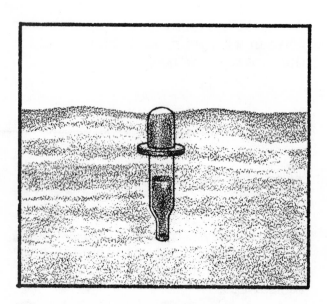

2. Next, let's fill the eyedropper with enough water so that the top just floats at the surface of the water.

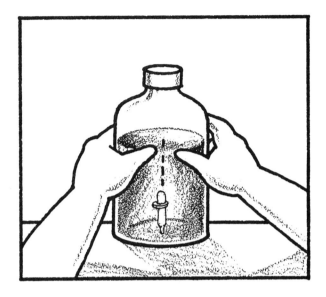

3. Let's put the eyedropper into the container and screw the lid on tight. Don't squeeze out any water!

4. Now squeeze the sides of the bottle with your hands and watch! What happens?

What Did You See?

When you squeezed the bottle, the eyedropper sank to the bottom! When you weren't squeezing the bottle, the eyedropper floated on top of the water.

Why Did It Happen?

When you squeeze the bottle, the space inside it gets smaller. The water pushes upward, but the air can't go anywhere, so it pushes the water back. The only place the water can go is up the eyedropper. And you know what happens when things get filled with water—they get heavy and sink!

The Big Squeeze

What You Need:

Plasticine clay; a 2-liter, clear plastic soft drink bottle with a cap; a cork that will fit the bottle snugly; a clear straw.

What To Do:

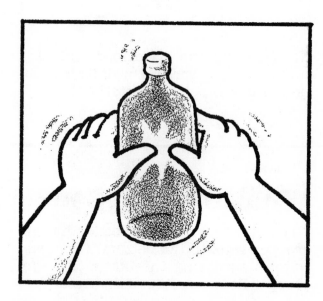

1. When you squeeze a piece of bread, it gets much smaller. But what happens when you squeeze water? Let's fill a bottle and leave the cap off, then squeeze the bottle. What happens?

2. Now put the cap on tightly. Squeeze! Squeeze hard! Well?

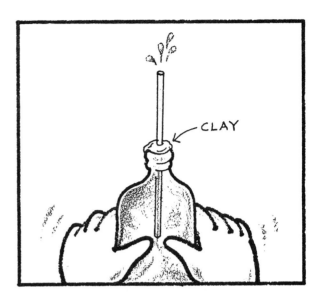

3. Try taking the cap off and putting a cork in the top. Now squeeze! What happens this time?

4. Mom or Dad will put a straw in the bottle, and then seal around the straw with clay. Now squeeze again!

What Did You See?

When you had the cap screwed on tightly, the water didn't come out, and you couldn't squeeze the bottle much at all! You could only squeeze it when there was a way for the water to come out—when there was no cap on, or when the water popped the cork off or went up the straw.

Why Did It Happen?

You can't make water any smaller. When you squeeze it, it has to go somewhere, so it squirts out of the bottle.

A Little Hole

Parent's Note:

Your kids might have already figured out the concept behind this activity. If they have, go on to the next one. If not, they'll learn something that has many practical applications. Some containers are made with a small hole near the spout to allow air in or out when the spout is filled with liquid. You can either make a hole in the bottle before you start and tape it over for the first 2 steps, or make the hole while you're doing the activity.

What You Need:

Plasticine clay; a 2-liter, clear plastic soft drink bottle or any other narrow-necked, clear plastic container; a funnel that fits the opening; a pitcher; a knife or scissors.

What To Do:

1. Try filling a bottle by using a pitcher and funnel. That's easy!

← CLAY

2. This time let's put clay around the funnel to seal it in the mouth of the bottle. Now try filling the bottle again. Notice any difference?

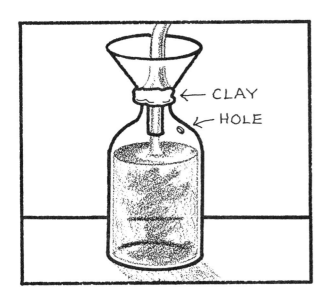

3. Next, Mom or Dad will put a little hole in the bottle near the main opening. Try to fill the bottle again. How does that work?

4. Now let Mom or Dad fill the bottle while you hold your finger over the hole and then lift it off! You can control the flow of the water.

What Did You See?

When you sealed the bottle, the water started to fill it up and then stopped. But when you put the little hole in the bottle, the water filled it right up!

Why Did It Happen?

The bottles that fill the fastest are the ones that let the air leave while the water is flowing in. If the air can't escape, then it takes up space in the bottle and won't let the water get in.

Stop the Leak

Parent's Note:

Sometimes a different perspective provides added insight. This activity, a follow-up to "A Little Hole," does just that. You can use the same container as before; just tape or cover the small hole at the top. Maybe this activity will remind you of those shopping trips when a milk carton has sprung a leak—a small one at that!

What You Need:

A 2-liter, clear plastic soft drink container with a cap; tape; a knife or scissors.

What To Do:

1. Let's fill a bottle, then put the cap on.

2. Let Mom or Dad poke a small hole in the bottom and watch carefully. What happens? Wiggle the container a bit. Does anything happen? Is there water coming out?

3. Now take the cap off, then put it back on. What happens to the leak?

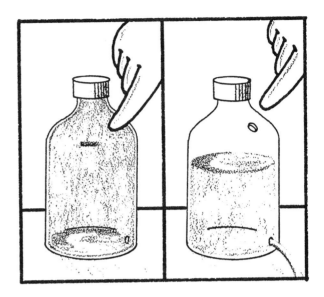

4. Next, have Mom or Dad make a little hole near the top. Put your finger over the hole, then take it off. What's happening?

What Did You See?

No water came out of the little hole on the bottom while the cap was on the bottle. But when you took the cap off or opened the little hole near the top, then the water started draining out.

Why Did It Happen?

When the top of the bottle is sealed, water doesn't drain out of the bottom because air can't get in to replace it. But as soon as air has a way to get in at the top, the water goes out the bottom.

Catching Bubbles

Parent's Note:

Encourage your child to include this activity with other bubble blowing. Catching bubbles can be as much fun as catching snowflakes. The bubble wands are the key: single-circle wands are best and wire ones seem better for "ringing" bubbles.

What You Need:

Bubble solution; 2 bubble wands.

What To Do:

1. Let's blow some bubbles. Try making little ones and big ones. Now dry your hand and try to catch a bubble. Is it easy or hard to do?

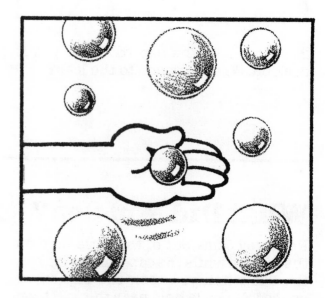

2. Try it again with a wet hand. Put some bubble soap on your hand. Is it any easier to catch bubbles now? Try catching one with your wand. What is the secret to catching bubbles?

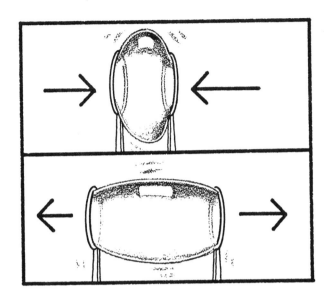

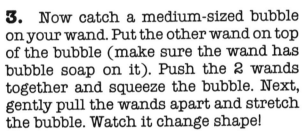

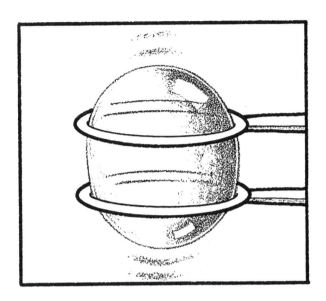

3. Now catch a medium-sized bubble on your wand. Put the other wand on top of the bubble (make sure the wand has bubble soap on it). Push the 2 wands together and squeeze the bubble. Next, gently pull the wands apart and stretch the bubble. Watch it change shape!

4. Now catch a bubble the same size as the hole in your bubble wand. Coat a second wand with soap (make sure it doesn't have a bubble stretched across it), then slide the second wand down over the bubble you caught on the first wand. Wow! You can "ring" the bubble.

What Did You See?

If your hand was wet with water or bubble soap, the bubbles didn't break as easily. When you coat your wand with soap, it slides over a bubble.

Why Did It Happen?

Soap helps water stretch and keep from drying out. When a soap bubble hits something dry, it dries out and pops. But when it touches something wet or soapy, it doesn't dry out as quickly, so it doesn't pop! Soap lets a bubble bend and stretch. The sides of a bubble change when you squeeze, stretch, or ring it, but the amount of air inside stays the same.

Bubble Chains

Keep the bubble solution handy—you're not done yet! If you're having a problem with the bubble solution tipping over, try putting it inside another container. This last bubble activity is the hardest. Encourage your child to keep trying.

What You Need:

Bubble solution; a bubble wand; a straw.

What To Do:

1. Let's try to make a bubble chain. First, blow a medium-sized bubble and catch it on your wand. Turn the wand so the bubble hangs below it.

2. Dip the straw in the bubble soap, and put it on the bottom of the bubble. Now blow gently and make another bubble. See how they stick together? Make a chain and try different sizes of bubbles.

3. Now blow one medium-sized bubble, catch it on your wand, and turn it upside down or help it come to rest on the side of the tub.

4. Dip the end of a straw in bubble soap and poke it in the center of the bubble. Now blow another bubble inside the first. It's not easy, so keep trying.

What Did You See?

The bubbles stuck to each other to form a chain. Sticking a wet straw into a bubble didn't break it—you could even blow another bubble inside the first one.

Why Did It Happen?

If you put them together very gently, bubbles will cling together. Bubble soap lets a straw pass into a bubble because the soap helps the bubble bend and stretch around the straw.

Siphon Secrets

What You Need:

A wide-mouthed, clear plastic container; a flexible plastic tube about 3 feet (or 1 meter) long and ½ inch (or 1 centimeter) in diameter.

What To Do:

1. You've seen what air pressure—the weight of the air—can do to water. Let's fill a container almost full and set it on the side of the tub. Be careful it doesn't tip over.

2. How can we use air pressure to get the water from the container into the tub without touching the container? Let's try one way called *siphoning*. Fill a tube with water and hold both ends so none spills out.

3. Now put one end of the tube in the container so the end of the tube touches the bottom of the container. Bend the other end down into the tub. Have Mom or Dad hold the container so it doesn't tip!

4. Watch what happens! Remember, the end of the tube in the tub has to be lower than the bottom of the container. Where is the water in the container going?

What Did You See?

The water from the container flowed up the tube and then down into the tub. Siphoning removed *all* the water from the container!

Why Did It Happen?

The tube is filled with water, so there is no room for air or air pressure in the tube. The air above the open container presses down on the water in the container, pushing the water up into the tube. Gravity and the water's own weight then pull the water down the tube and into the bathtub.

Up the Wall

Parent's Note:

Water moves upward when it is siphoned and when it is seeking its own level. In "Siphon Secrets," it was being pushed up the tube by air pressure. In this activity, water will move upward because of *capillary action*, the tendency of water to travel upward in thin tubes and porous materials. This is how water gets from the roots of a tree to the leaves.

What You Need:

A small plastic cup; tape; a marking pen; strips of paper towel.

What To Do:

1. We've seen how water is pushed upward by air pressure in a siphon tube. Another way that water can go upward is called *capillary action*. Let's try it! First, fill a cup of water and set it on the corner of the tub.

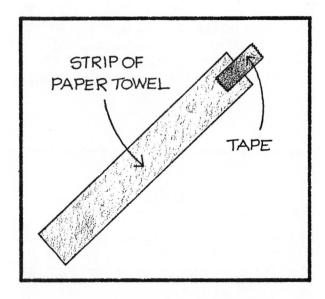

STRIP OF PAPER TOWEL

TAPE

2. Now let's take a strip of paper towel and put a piece of tape on one end.

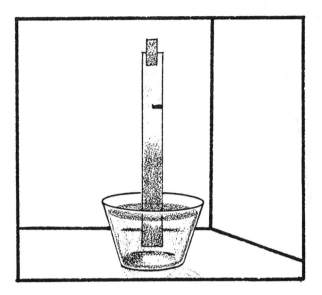

3. In a minute we're going to put one end of the paper towel into the water in the cup and tape the other end to the wall above it. You know that water soaks into a paper towel, but will it really soak straight upward? Put a mark on the towel as high as you think the water will go.

4. Now put one end of the paper towel in the water and tape the other to the wall above the cup. Keep an eye on the paper towel while you're taking your bath. Is the water moving up the paper towel? Be patient!

What Did You See?

The water moved upward and soaked into the paper towel.

Why Did It Happen?

Water likes to stick to fibers and other materials. Wherever the water touches other materials, it clings to that material and reaches upward, trying to get a better grasp. Once the water on the sides gets a grasp, it pulls more water from the middle upward. Water can creep up a small tube just like an inchworm going up a tree!

Cloth Siphon

Parent's Note:

This last demonstration of water going up-hill combines capillary action with siphoning. The key is to use a small cloth that rests on the bottom of the higher container and the top of the lower. Leaving this siphon overnight produces some dramatic results!

What You Need:

A medium-sized plastic container; a small bowl; a wooden block that you can set the container on and that's as high as the bowl; a handkerchief.

What To Do:

1. Let's try using siphoning and capillary action to empty a plastic container without touching it! Fill the container with water and set it on the wooden block. Now place a bowl next to it.

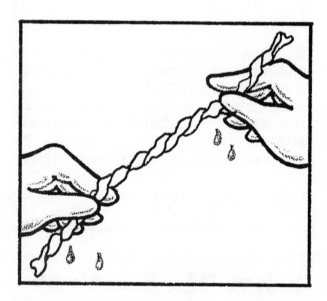

2. Wet the handkerchief and wring it out. Leave it twisted like a rope.

3. Put one end of the handkerchief in the plastic container so it touches the bottom. (It's OK if the cloth is long and you have to push it into the container.) Put the other end in the bowl so the tip *barely* hangs over the edge.

4. Now go on with your bath! Check once when your bath is over and again tomorrow. What happens to the water?

What Did You See?

The handkerchief slowly siphoned the water from the plastic container into the bowl.

Why Did It Happen?

The water soaks through the cloth a little at a time because of capillary action. Remember how water rose to the top of the paper towel in "Up the Wall?" This time water rises to the top of the cloth, then the weight of the water pulls it down through the cloth into the bowl.

String Me Along

Parent's Note:

Moving water from one place to another is our focus once again. Make sure you use *exactly* the materials listed if you want this to work! The key is to have a 3-foot (1-meter) string that can absorb water. Cotton string is best—nylon string or wool yarn will not work well. The pitcher also needs a small spout to funnel the water in a stream. You'll soon know the secret to pouring from one container into another a good distance away. (Be careful, this could be messy.)

What You Need:

A pitcher with a handle and a small spout or pouring lip; a wide-mouthed, clear plastic container; a piece of cotton string about 3 feet (or 1 meter) long.

What To Do:

1. Do you think a string can be used to fill a container with water? Let's find out! First set an empty container on the side of the tub and fill a pitcher with water.

2. Next, we'll dip a string in the tub water and tie one end to the handle of the pitcher.

3. Stretch the wet string across the top of the pitcher and over to the empty container. Hold the free end over the container.

4. Now, *carefully* pour the water out of the pitcher so the water runs onto the wet string. What does the water do?

What Did You See?

The water followed the string and dripped off the end into the empty container.

Why Did It Happen?

The water from the pitcher clings to the water on the string. The weight of the water pushes it down toward the empty container. The water clings so tightly to the wet string that it doesn't drop off until it reaches the end!

Look Again

Parent's Note:

Your kids probably already know how the curved surface of a drop of water acts like a magnifying glass. In fact, they may already have commented that their feet look bigger under the water than above it. Let your children experiment with different clear plastic containers and see what distortions and magnifications occur.

What You Need:

A tall, narrow, clear plastic container; some square or rectangular clear plastic containers; a ruler.

What To Do:

1. Water can make things look bigger than they really are. Look at your toes under the water. Now lift them above the water. See any difference? Not much, but some!

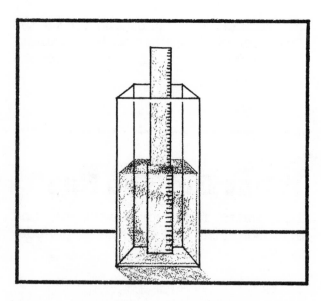

2. Now let's fill a tall, thin container half full. Put a ruler in it so that half of it is above the water and half of it is below. Look down into the container. See any difference?

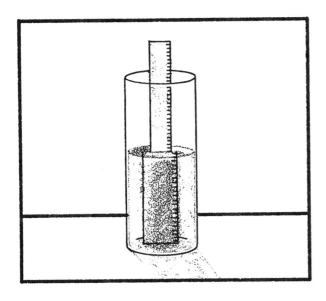

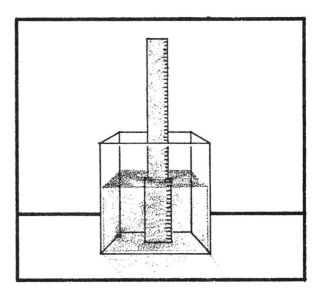

3. Let's try it with a round container. How does the ruler look now—bigger or smaller?

4. This time let's use a square container. Do things look as large in square containers as they do in round ones?

What Did You See?

The ruler looked biggest in the tall, curved container. Containers with flat sides don't make things look much bigger.

Why Did It Happen?

The water and the curved surface of the container both act like lenses or magnifying glasses. They make whatever is placed inside them look bigger. The container alone doesn't make things look bigger; it's a combination of the water *and* the container.

Order Form

Quantity	Title	Author	Order No.	Unit Cost	Total
	A Hundred Scoops of Ice Cream	Josefowitz, N.	2280	$3.95	
	1,2,3...Play with me!	Paré, R.	2240	$12.95	
	A,B,C...Play with me!	Paré, R.	2230	$12.95	
	Baby & Child Medical Care	Hart, T.	1159	$6.95	
	Dear Babysitter	Lansky, V.	1059	$8.95	
	Dino Dots	Dixon, D.	2250	$4.95	
	Dictionary According to Mommy	Armor, J.	4110	$4.95	
	Discipline Without Shouting or Spanking	Wyckoff/Unell	1079	$5.95	
	Do They Ever Grow Up?	Johnston, L.	1089	$4.95	
	Feed Me! I'm Yours	Lansky, V.	1109	$6.95	
	Learn While You Scrub, Science in the Tub	Lewis, J.	2350	$6.95	
	Mother Murphy's Law	Lansky, B.	1149	$3.50	
	Practical Parenting Tips	Lansky, V.	1179	$6.95	
	Rub-a-Dub-Dub, Science in the Tub	Lewis, J.	2270	$5.95	
	Stork didn't bring me	Hébert, M.	2220	$12.95	

Meadowbrook Press

Subtotal	
Shipping and Handling (see below)	
MN residents add 6% sales tax	
Total	

YES, please send me the books indicated above. Add $1.25 shipping and handling for the first book and $.50 for each additional book. Add $1.75 for each Read & Play Learning Set. Add $2.00 to total for books shipped to Canada. Overseas postage will be billed. Allow up to 4 weeks for delivery. Send check or money order payable to Meadowbrook Press. No cash or C.O.D.'s please. Quantity discounts available upon request. Prices subject to change without notice.

Send book(s) to:

Name_____

Address_____

City_____ State_____ Zip_____

☐ Check enclosed for $_____, payable to Meadowbrook Press
☐ Charge to my credit card (for purchases of $10.00 or more only)
☐ Phone Orders call: (800) 338-2232 (for purchases of $10.00 or more only)

Account #_____ ☐ Visa ☐ MasterCard

Signature_____ Exp. date_____

Meadowbrook Press, 18318 Minnetonka Boulevard, Deephaven, MN 55391 (612) 473-5400